THE CHRIST CONSCIOUSNESS
A Somewhat Agnostic Point-of-View

Sue Beckley

Copyright ©2022 Quantum Explorations

All rights reserved. This book or any portion thereof may not be reproduced or used in any manner whatsoever without the express written permission of the publisher except for the use of brief quotations in a book review.

www.quantumexplorations.com

The Christ Consciousness cover art, typesetting, and editing done by Brent Beckley.

Printed and bound in the United States of America.

All authors mentioned are real and recommended.

Quantum Explorations
Leesburg, Florida, USA

ISBN: 979-8-218-04159-5

10 9 8 7 6 5 4 3 2 1

DEDICATION and ACKNOWLEDGMENTS

My spiritual, self-love journey began about 30 years ago. Brent Beckley has been with me throughout, supporting me and loving me through all of the versions of myself that I have opened up to. I will always be eternally grateful for the presence of this beautiful soul in my life. This book is dedicated to Brent with thanks, and much love.

Erika Furuzono is a dear friend, an excellent quantum healer and life coach, and has worked with me for the past two years spreading the messages of The Christ Consciousness as we have discovered it within us, and through sessions, to share with others as they search for it. I appreciate our co-creationship and Erika's unwavering ability and willingness to help me decipher the messages. I look forward to finding more of my truths and opening up to the higher vibrational energies with Erika.

Pier Bene is a cherished friend and fellow quantum healer who I have been lucky enough to meet and work with as we both searched for answers about The Christ Consciousness. I look forward to further explorations with Pier, and our co-creationship as it continues to unfold.

TABLE OF CONTENTS

Introduction	1
Source	9
Why Separation?	17
What is the Christ Consciousness?	21
How Many Higher Selves Do We Have?	25
Expectations and The Christ Consciousness	33
Helping	37
Creation Through The Christ Consciousness	41
Your Body	45
Forgiveness and Release	51
Gratitude	59
The All	61
Conclusion	65

INTRODUCTION

Hello! My name is Sue Beckley, and this book is designed to share my journey and understanding of embodying the energy that has been called The Christ Consciousness. The first question any person might ask is, "What makes this Sue Beckley an expert enough to write a book about The Christ Consciousness?" Excellent question!

I will tell you right away that I am not an expert. I am not a teacher. I am a fellow traveler within the Earth experience who has spent the last 30+ years of my life dedicated to understanding myself and human behavior, learning all that I am capable of absorbing about the truths of the Universe and life here, and someone who has discovered some meaning of The Christ Consciousness along the way.

I think this information could be helpful to others; as it has been for me. I wish to share it. And really, isn't that what most of us do with helpful information? We like to share it. I've noticed that sharing is a 'key' component within the communities that I have felt the most connected to on my Earth journey.

Why do I call it a journey? Another good question. And I promise to answer this question in a little while when I talk about Source. First, I would like to speak about the title of this book, specifically, the "A Somewhat Agnostic Point of View" part. What is agnostic? This is the definition that I found that makes sense to me: "...a person who holds that the existence of the ultimate cause, as God, and the essential nature of things are unknown and unknowable, or that human knowledge is limited to experience."

When I included the word "Somewhat" in the title, it is because I agree with the definition above where it states that human knowledge is limited to experience. I do not agree that the existence of God is unknowable. I call God "Source." You may call it whatever you wish because what we humans know as God/Source has been called by many names. The term agnostic is helpful because I **really** want to appeal to the masses with this information. All people, from every walk of life, because I do not believe that The Christ Consciousness is limited to Christians. What kind of God would give energy gifts (or any gifts) to one group of its creations and not all of them?

I'm going to be honest with you and state that I believe that religions have been created over time by humans, and thus no one religion has all the answers. Religions hold many truths. And if you sort through them, as I have, these truths can be known (felt). But, religion is not the only way to know God. Some religions have been altered over time to suit agendas of mankind, and thus the original purpose of those religions have been skewed from the pure intent that created them. This dialogue and sharing is NOT going to get into that topic. The topic of religion and the arguments that follow are an exercise in what we spiritualists call separation from Source, and this book is not about separation. It is about Unity Consciousness, which is The Christ Consciousness. I know, I know, you have heard all that before. It sounds like spiritual mumbo jumbo. Many of us have heard it so many times that it seems to be a buzz phrase. I will attempt, through this sharing, to give you many concrete examples of my understanding of The Christ Consciousness so that you; the one investing your precious time with this book, can get something out of it more than buzz words and phrases.

Back to agnosticism. My "somewhat agnostic" descriptions of The Christ Consciousness are going to expand way beyond the definitions of any religion, and they will touch on some definitions that you will find within religious texts.

I can't help that.

The sharing that I do with you through my writing is a

conglomeration of my life experiences. I've read so many books by so many authors that have described spiritual concepts and religious concepts that I have become an embodiment of the ones that made sense to me! And this is an especially important thing for you to remember as you read this. Anything and everything I will say to you is **subject to your own filters**.

We all have filters with which we interpret life and meaning. Our filters are created through everything we have experienced, and everything we have been told is truth. Filters can be like what psychologists would call "defense mechanisms." Basically, filters are a set of invisible glasses that we wear throughout life that allow us to process the information that comes to us in every moment of living life. And so, filters are neither good nor bad, they just are. Filters can be altered, or changed completely as we navigate life. Our filters are based on our beliefs. And if we are open to changing our beliefs when new information comes in, because that information makes sense to us, then our filters change automatically. It is not a concept I wish to burden you with. My hope here is to make you aware that we all have filters, our filters may be similar to others, but your filter is unique to any other person's filter, and so this book will affect you uniquely. And this is why I use the term agnostic in the way that I defined.

Our life **experiences** determine what is truth, and what is not. As my mentor said to me many years ago, "take what has meaning to you, and disregard the rest." What he meant by that is; through our discussions, he offered me his truths. But he never assumed that his truths should become mine. My mentor, Bob, was wise enough to know that I would have to find my own truths in life and that his sharing of his truths could be helpful, because I asked him to share them. Bob recognized that the act of my asking meant that he had some information within him to share, which might be useful for me to hear. The same for you and choosing this book to read. We are "called" to read the texts and sharing of information when the time for that information to be processed by us has come. Some call that Divine timing, or synchronicity. I say there are no accidents in life. If you chose this book, then there is something in it for you. Hopefully a few somethings! Please take from it what has meaning for you and disregard the rest.

And now to tell you a bit about me. One thing I do and have done for five years is quantum healing. Quantum healing is when someone accesses universal energies to heal the mind, body, spirit, and emotional bodies. These universal energies are available at all times, and from every dimension. Some of the energies that we encounter during a quantum healing session have bodies and are incarnated on another planet, but most are etheric energies (your guides, your higher selves, angels, ancestors, Source). My job as a QHHT and BQH practitioner is to hypnotize the client, which is a way of saying: 'to get them very relaxed using guided meditation and visualization, for the purpose of shifting their thinking mind to inactive, or very relaxed; and then open the feeling and intuitive mind, to universal energies, to receive information and healing.'

That is a mouthful, but what I really just said is that I help people calm their minds and shift from left brained "thinking" to right brained "intuiting," for the purpose of accessing information and energy. I practice Delores Cannon's Quantum Healing Hypnosis Technique (QHHT) and Candace Craw-Goldman's Beyond Quantum Healing (BQH). Candace was a student of Delores, and became a teacher with Delores. I was attracted to Candace's teachings which, in my opinion, expanded Delores' work and encouraged all healing practitioners of any modality to commune with Delores's method, and create sessions for people that are multifaceted. So, if I have the ability of claircognizance (I do), and I am an empath (I am), I can combine these abilities with the hypnosis techniques of QHHT to give the client a more comprehensive session.

For example, if someone I'm working with tells me that they 'can't visualize,' then I'm going to use my empathic ability to feel for what the issue is. Are they fearful of what they might see during a session? Do they feel closed off to sharing their 'secrets' for me to hear? These two scenarios require different approaches for me as a practitioner. Reading a hypnosis script for every client is not going to work in all cases. Even my experience as a former social worker gets incorporated into my sessions. I can tell if a client needs more time talking about themselves in the pre-session or when a client is ready to get going and dive into the session. And so, I use my personal abilities to assist the client in their endeavor to become hypnotized and combine them with the hypnosis techniques I have learned from Delores and Candace. This usually leads the client to the healing and answers that they were seeking by having a session. Some BQH practitioners are energy workers. They are trained in Reiki, EFT, Restorative Touch or another similar practice for energy healing. I practice both QHHT and BQH, mixed with my own healing talents.

Being a quantum healer has opened my own consciousness tremendously. I had a session done for myself by another QHHT practitioner before I chose to study the practice. I wanted to see if I could contact my higher-self. At the time, my understanding was that we all have a higher-self, in a higher vibrational dimension (hence the name), that is not incarnated, but watches over us and guides us in our lives. I wanted to meet my higher-self. And boy did I! I also received energetic healing (translates to the physical) of my heart, which I didn't know was weak at the time from all the heartaches I had sustained in my life. Under hypnosis (again, just an altered state of mind/consciousness), I witnessed my own heart being shown to me while energy (golden and white rays of light) surrounded it and healed it. I felt the energy. It is difficult to describe, but it was a whole-body experience. And it only took seconds for the healing to take place! I felt amazing! I was also ill at the time with a flu-like sickness, and after my session, my flu symptoms were gone. I had lots of energy and I replayed the images and messages I received over and over in my mind to fully comprehend and institute the changes that my higher-self suggested that I make in my life.

This is the key to quantum healing. A client can get all the information and healing they ask for, **but if that client doesn't implement the advice given in the session, that client will most likely return to the former conditions that were healed during the session.** Healing really is an internal job no matter what healing modality or medical practice a person chooses for themselves. I think Einstein said something about trying to solve a problem using the same methods over and over again and expecting to get different results. Some people call that the definition of stupidity, but I say that we each have done this, many times, because we are programmed by our families and society to think and do things a certain way. It was not our family's intention, nor society's, to mislead us. But we need to advance our consciousness by realizing that not every person benefits from the same advice. One size healing doesn't fit all. Once you get clarity from a quantum healing session about how to change YOUR life, it is then up to you to do it, or not.

Personal responsibility.

I'm all about that. And personal power! This is what I teach, if anything, through my quantum healing practice. Being in direct contact with the higher dimensional energies of a quantum healing session, whether I'm giving one or receiving one, has opened my consciousness up to more comprehensive understandings than any information that I have read in a book. I have read probably hundreds of spiritual books over thirty years. And sometimes these sessions confirmed information that I have read about in books, but I merely knew the information from the books as a concept. Once you know something and then experience that something; then you can implement that something into your life until it is a part of you, like breathing. And then that something becomes internalized. The energies of the higher dimensions of the universe are available to every single soul, and all you need to do is ask and listen for the answers.

Many people find their own answers through meditation and silence while asking their guides, God/Source, ancestors or angels; questions. During their silence, the answers may be heard, felt, seen or known. Other people need a sort of in-between method to get to that place, like consulting a psychic or having a quantum healing session. Whatever way you choose to connect to universal forces is fine. All ways of getting information for your highest good are fine. My way to understanding the concepts I will share with you has come through quantum healing primarily, mixed with other life experiences (practice), and wisdom I have gleaned from other human beings that have been kind enough to share.

In conclusion to this introduction, I will say that I AM. I am of Source, **and so are you**. I speak to you as a fellow traveler of Earth (journeyer), as an aspect of the Divine (and so are you), and as a friend.

SOURCE

We must start talking about Source before we get into discussion about The Christ Consciousness. Why? Because Source is where The Christ Consciousness emanates from. This is also the case with everything, everyone, and every concept that has ever been thought of or created. Source can be thought of as a consciousness, or an energy. Or an energy with consciousness. I can't say nor define what Source is in its entirety because, here we go again, I'm somewhat agnostic, and limited to my experiences. I can share my understanding with you.

Source knows all. And at some point, Source decided to experience itself differently from knowing by having physical experience (journeying). Remember I said earlier that knowing and experiencing are not the same? Source had a question for itself. "What would it be like to be **not** Source?" And so aspects of Source separated (journeyed) from the whole and into these energy groupings that some humans call monads (similar to what is called a "soul group"). Aspects of Source within the monad have their own unique energy signatures, but **always** contain the spark of Source within them. The thing with the monads is that they separated from Source, but they still realize consciously that they are a part of Source and could go back to the whole of Source at any time.

That dimensional distance from Source does not feel much different to being Source. This brought about another question within the monads. "How far away from Source can we go?" This question needed more experiences to explore the answers (more journeying). How would anyone know for sure an answer about something unless they experienced it? Could you know what an alcoholic goes through if you've never been an alcoholic? You might be able to think about what it would be like, but you would never **know** unless you experienced it.

The monads set about creation of universes, stars, and worlds. Energy, condensed through density, into matter. Matter and form were created through the conscious manipulation of energy by the monads, brought about by the questioning. Source is in total agreement with this journeying because as I mentioned earlier, Source seeks to know itself through experience, not just being All-knowing. Many levels of density of energy were created, and we call them dimensions. Energy in one dimensional vibration can and does behave differently in another dimension. Think gas, liquid, solid. The energy of us (that we call a soul) can be non-corporeal in the higher dimensions because the vibration of that energy is too light to hold a physical form. When that energy decides to lower its frequency, it sends a part of itself into lower density, and becomes form (incarnated). This is what happens when souls come into bodies and leave them again. It is not a death of any kind, just a transition of states of being. This is why you can hear, see, smell and feel your deceased relatives. They are not gone, only transitioned to another conscious reality and state of energy vibration. They try to communicate with us when we could use some help, or need to feel supported by them. When we can see, hear, feel or smell them, that means we have reached a state of higher vibration than we normally hold with our five senses. Our ancestors (deceased) have to lower their energy to reach us from their current state of vibration. Sometimes they cannot vibrate low enough to reach us and therefore, **we must be the ones who increase our vibrations if we want to contact them**.

All of this back and forth from non-body to incarnated, is a series of journeys. Souls like to journey from one reality to another, and through all of the dimensions. Theses journeys help Source to experience all possible iterations of itself, through each aspect's journey, and through each aspect's own perceptions.

Everyone's lives become a conglomeration of experience for Source, from every angle and perception possible. If we all had the same perception, we wouldn't have much of a journey, and the experiences would not be as expansive for Source as they are.

Source's aspects (us) continued to create more realities to explore in. Many densities were created because different density realities allow us to have more diverse experiences. A quantum playground, if you will, of experiences for Source to discover itself entirely. Once Source's aspects got to the lowest densities, they forgot who they were and where they came from because their consciousness's became limited. One can never get too far from Source as to be **disconnected** from Source, but the conscious awareness of one who has journeyed to a distant dimensional vibration can be very limited, to the point of forgetting. And we call this the Veil of Forgetting when we talk about Earth. Now, here's a really important thing to remember. Do you recall that I said that each aspect of Source carries within it the spark of Source? This spark, which resides in ALL of us, is the exact same energy of Source as a whole. Like a clone. No one's spark is more special than another's. It is within us, all the time, no matter how much forgetting we do. The darkest deeds a person could ever do will never erase the spark of Source within themselves.

Some aspects of Source decided to never incarnate, but rather remained in the higher dimension of the monads and they look after those of us that do incarnate. Those we call angels. Angels are referred to in Judaism, Zoroastrianism, Christianity, and Islam as "angels." In other belief systems, these beings are referred to by other names. Angels are not relegated to serve only those who believe in religion. They serve us all, even when we are unaware of their existence or deny their existence. I use the term "angels" because it is just easier than trying to come up with a new term that most people won't recognize.

How long this has been going on? I will answer by telling you that there is no time. All of this infinite experience (or journeying), spirals back onto itself in a continuous loop, which creates multiple, deeper opportunities to experience all possible definitions of separation from source. Time is a factor of linear reality that helps us keep our place in life on Earth, so that we can feel we are moving towards something. We use time to calculate progress because we see events in time as a measure for comparison. Possibly to measure our progress in our mission on Earth, I'm not sure. In the density of 3D consciousness, our human brains are not able to hold multiple realities at the same "time" and not go crazy. We call people who experience multidimensional realities and have difficulty processing those realities, schizophrenic, and lock them up or drug them so that they can be more linear like the rest of us.

Earth has been known as a third dimensional planet. This dimensional vibration is dense, and as mentioned earlier, we have forgotten our connection to Source. It is time for Earth, our universe, and all aspects of Source within (including ETs) to shift and grow our consciousness to the fifth dimensional consciousness, as our games of separation have been played out. As we move from the 3rd dimension to the 5th, our vibration is rising (becoming faster) and our consciousness expands. Many call this ascension. I say it is remembering who and what we really are. This consciousness expansion allows us to hold the concepts of multiple realities as possible, and it allows us to know that we create reality rather than thinking that anything we are experiencing is by chance. As aspects of Source, we are creators, just like Source. Nothing and no one in your experience is happening by accident. You have, in agreement with other souls, chosen this reality and created it. Earth and all of the planets in our Universe are created as free-will planets. That means that no thing or soul "outside" of you can force you to do anything! Even when it seems you are the victim of some outside entity or person, it is because you agreed upon this action, before you incarnated, to have the experience. This we call a soul contract.

I know, that's a tough pill to swallow. What about rape, incest, sickness, murder, infant death and every other horrible experience you can think of? Yes, all of it. We choose our life plan according to what our soul wishes to experience next, and other souls also wishing to have that experience agree to play roles in our reality so that we may experience it. Please read the works of Robert Schwartz on this topic if it does not make any sense to you. He spent many years researching it, working with many people during that research, and there is no way I can present this information any better than he did. May I suggest his book: *Your Soul's Gift; The Healing Power of the Life You Planned Before You Were Born.*

Source does not judge itself for what it wishes to experience. You are a part of Source, and so, Source does not judge you. Please get that firmly ingrained into your mind. It will serve you as I share more about The Christ Consciousness. For that matter, it is essential for you to accept this statement of non-judgement if you want to embody The Christ Consciousness. I will say more about that as we go on.

Everything that each aspect of Source experiences becomes part of the record and memory of Source. All of it. From the goings on of a fly to the water that flows. The consciousness of each being, whether considered "alive" or "inanimate," flows to Source. There are group consciousnesses (collectives), and individual consciousness. Individual consciousness applies to each soul's journey until that soul joins a collective, before going back to Source. Yes, flies and animals have souls, and so do the rocks and furniture. Their consciousness operates differently from humans, but everything has one. Some people can relate better with an example.

Let's say we think about a house. The house is comprised of all the energy of the materials it was built with, and the energy of the designers and builders, plus the energy of the Earth it was built upon. Then someone comes along and lives in the house. These people give their energy to it. Life goes on inside and outside of that house, and the house absorbs that energy, which becomes part of the house's consciousness (collective consciousness). Now the house isn't actively thinking about what goes on inside of it or who built it, nor the energy of the tree that helped create it. The house as a whole has absorbed and recorded these energies. This type of consciousness is not the thinking kind.

When you step into the house, you can feel its energy. Some people who are sensitive to energy and are not solely focused on appearances can walk into a house and feel if the house has been a happy environment, or they can feel trauma that a house has had within it, and every shade of gray in-between. Everything is made of energy, consciousness is energy, and souls are energy. And so, everything has consciousness. It may not be the kind of consciousness that can hold a conversation with you, but **Source understands all**, and does not invalidate any consciousness that it is being (the act being). Source records all.

Fun factoid, this is how psychics (energy readers) can find out information about you through an object that you wear or carry around with you. Psychics are energy readers. Just as an empath feels energy, a psychic can read your energy and tell you things about your past, present, and future timelines. Your past, present and future are all going on at the same "time," which means that these energies are available to be read by anyone, with permission. Remember free will. It is not advisable to try to read people without their permission because that is intrusive and violates free will. Many psychics will ask you if you give them permission to read your energy, and that is respectful, but the act of coming in for a reading is permission. You also give permission to other people to read your energy when you come to them for advice or share your stories on social media. You are giving them access to your energy fields. Something to consider.

Source doesn't care what you call it. We are it, and so whatever name you wish to use, Source understands that you are calling upon it, and responds, always. There is no one more worthy of response from Source than you. There is no person that has attained a stature worthy of Source more than you. Source is everywhere, supporting all creation (itself). Source loves us all in equal measure. Yes, even the ones you think are "evil." Why is it then, that Source allows such a difference between good and evil? Why is evil allowed at all? Good question! The answer is, because Source needed to create separation (the good and the bad) in order to experience what it is like to be "not-Source." I will cover separation in the next chapter.

A final word about Source, and possibly the most important thing I can say about it. Source is the vibrational energy of unconditional love. Period. Anything that appears to be other than love, not-Source, is an illusion of separation. I believe John Lennon had it right when he sang "all you need is love."

WHY SEPARATION?

Separation is a term commonly used in these times by practitioners of spiritualism. It means: all conditions that appear to be separate from love (other than love), or, believing that we are separate from God/Source instead of knowing that we are all aspects of Source, having individual journeys. In other words, all things that **do not seem to be love**. Source aspects could not journey to explore what it is like to be "not-Source" if everything felt like love. The monads (groups of aspects of Source, or soul groups) stretched out their creations farther and farther away from Source, dimensionally/vibrationally, until they created forms and realities that forgot what Source is, and that they are aspects of it. One such creation is the Earth.

Earth was originally created in the 5th density, with humans that carried higher consciousnesses, which means that they still had their memories of being of Source. Earth descended to the 3rd density eventually because souls wanted their human counterparts to go deeper into separation where they played deeper games of separation. Rather than behaving as a community, and helping one another out because it benefits the whole, they played games like; exercising power and control over each other, ownership of the land, and accumulation of material things as a measure of self-worth.

These games are even farther away from Source's vibration of unconditional love, and as humanity played them, they felt more real than games or journeys of exploration. The journey into 3D has lasted a long time. Humans took Mother Earth, or

Gaia, down into 3D with their games. Pollution, war, misuse of Mother Earth's gifts to humanity, and her absorbing of the density of 3D humans has threatened her to near destruction. Remember, everything has consciousness. And so does the Earth. This is why she is named. Gaia is the soul of the Earth that graciously volunteered to serve humanity by providing all that we need to live and experience our journeys. She has been sorely mistreated for her efforts, and yet she also has the personal power and consciousness to heal herself through all of humanity's abuse. More on Gaia later.

Separation: or the forgetting that we are all aspects of Source, The One, The All, has allowed us to explore just how far we could go being **not-Source**, while still having conscious awareness of ourselves as individuals. What does that mean? An example I will use is worms. Worms have consciousness, but it is limited to the functions of their biology. The consciousness of worms does not extend to thoughts of "other" or even "self." Worms live by instinct, and so do not think about anything. You could not channel a worm and ask it how it is feeling or what kind of day it is having. The worm only knows what it must do and has no concept of death. All impulses are due to its automatic nervous system and reactions to heat, cold and rain. One could consider such a consciousness as being two dimensional (2D). How do I know this about worms? Read the works of Arn Allingham, aka Zingdad, on Zingdad.com. His work is provided for free in PDF form. Or take my word for it. If humanity had sunk any lower in vibration than 3D, we would be like the worms and our consciousness could not even play the games that we sought to play to discover what it is to be non-Source. It would be only existing in a form without thought. The souls of humans could not see a benefit to that.

The souls of humanity want to explore being not-Source through good and bad, right and wrong, and the various levels in-between, but these souls understand that going any further past 3D was not going to render helpful lessons for soul growth. I think it is safe to say that killing, greed, stealing, cheating, lying, hierarchy of importance, betrayal and war are about the darkest, furthest away from unconditional love, that humanity needed to explore. These are the games of separation. A decision was made by all of us, on the soul level and as a collective, that the Earth journey has exhausted all the ways that we could be horrible to each other, and to experience the horrors. We have seen how far away from knowing ourselves as Source that we could be without losing our conscious awareness of self. Human souls began to cry out for love again. Deep inside, we knew that we didn't want to journey anymore in a world where these behaviors were perpetuated by other humans, to other humans, and Mother Earth. And so, we journey now back to remembering who and what we are. Source. We are ascending back, through our increased vibration, to remembering that we are All One, we are of Source, and to feel what it is like to experience unconditional love once again. We do this individually, and as a collective, by sharing what we remember. Spirituality is not about being separate, although it recognizes that each aspect of the One (Source) has something to share with the others towards reuniting as One once again. The exploration of separation is done now. Humanity has decided to go back the other way. This is ascension, or the great collective remembering.

WHAT IS THE CHRIST CONSCIOUSNESS?

The Christ Consciousness is the energy and vibration, the consciousness, that is our eternal connection to Source. It is the way that we think, believe, and behave that allows us **to be** the unconditional love that Source is, and bring it here, into our reality. The embodiment of The Christ Consciousness creates:

- heaven
- paradise
- nirvana
- hereafter
- beyond bliss
- empyrean
- afterlife
- afterworld
- above utopia
- atmosphere
- dreamland
- fairyland
- fantasyland
- sky
- Avalon
- Camelot
- Canaan
- Eden
- Elysium
- eternity
- heights
- immortality
- kingdom
- lotusland
- Sion
- Swarga upstairs
- Valhalla
- Zion
- Cockaigne
- kingdom come
- Promised Land
- Elysian Fields
- New Jerusalem
- City of God
- next world
- Shangri-la
- celestial city
- the blue heavenly kingdom
- kingdom of heaven
- life everlasting
- eternal home

and brings it manifest to Earth. I used all the terms I could find from the peoples of the Earth to define heaven, because as you can see, the non-religious know what I'm talking about too. That is the best definition I can give you. The Christ Consciousness is also referred to as Unity Consciousness, or the collective mind. It is easier for me to describe The Christ Consciousness (CC from here) and provide examples of it than to define it. All of The CC can be reached and embodied by all of Source's creations. It is my understanding and belief that Jesus' mission here on Earth was to remind humanity of that spark within them that is Source. His energy is still doing that from the dimension he is in, all these years after his "death." Being with humanity, as a part of it, Jesus became the embodiment of unconditional love.

Yes, Jesus was human, and displayed human emotions. And his vibration allowed anyone to feel their own connection to God/Source. Jesus' teachings were an effort to bring the CC within all of us into humanity's conscious awareness, to help us remember the truth, that we, like he; are all sons and daughters of the father.

Doesn't that sound a lot like we are aspects of Source?

We are All One?

Didn't Jesus tell us that what we do to another we also do to God? And didn't Jesus also say that everything he could do we also can do? Why is that?

Are we all parts of God? Indeed we are.

And **Jesus** is not the only soul who came to Earth to give humanity that reminder! Check any religious or spiritual practice and you find many examples of souls that came to Earth to help humanity learn to embody the CC. So many prophets. So many gurus. So many souls that came, as Jesus did, to help humanity remember.

What does embodiment mean? The CC is the eternal connection to Source, that spark that resides within us, that allows us to remember that if we are to start living the feelings and behaviors of unconditional love, we will align with Source, and we will embody it. Embodying something is to live it through your beliefs, words and actions. Humans have the CC within us, all the time. We have forgotten who we are for the most part, but we can witness the spark in everyday acts of kindness and sharing with others. People welcome other people's children into their homes and treat them as their own, people donate goods, services, and other resources to help strangers in need, people rush into burning buildings at their own risk to save others from perishing, people take care of the planet and its creatures, people listen to each other and lend their presence even when they don't know what to say. Everyday examples can be found of the CC if we look and intend to see them.

I'm going to go back to Jesus for a minute because I resonate with him the most. I remembered, through a quantum healing session, that I had a lifetime on Earth where I was an Essene. I was a male and a scribe of the information about Jesus (Jeshua). During this lifetime as the scribe, I met eyes with Jesus while he was carrying the cross to his crucifixion. I had never met Jesus before this moment. I traveled to be with Jesus during his final moments. I was in the crowd lined along the street, with tears in my eyes and a deep sorrow in my chest. The instant our eyes met, I saw and remembered who I am. Part of Source. Needless to say, even though I had been writing the stories of Jesus and knew of his power, I was rendered speechless for weeks after our eyes met. He saw into my soul, and transmitted the energy of The CC to me. He was able to assist me to see in myself my own God-spark. This is the meaning of Namaste! Namaste, a Hindi greeting, means "the God in me sees the God in you."

This story brings about one of the most important messages I can ever deliver. The CC within all of us can be shared, or it can be denied. We share it unconsciously all the time and call it kindness, or love. We share our energy with those around us, and those not around us (in the collective energy of humanity) by being. What we believe, say, feel and do are all states of our beingness. We can be consciously, or we can be unconsciously. Are we paying attention to what our beingness does to ourselves and other people? That is conscious **being**. If we keep doing things and feeling things and believing things without ever considering what they do to our lives and the people we love, or humanity, then that is unconscious being. Source doesn't care which state of being that we choose, conscious or unconscious. But our souls care. We want to remember completely, and end our separation from Source. We want to bring heaven to Earth. We want to live in community, harmony, mutual trust and respect. We want to BE love. We are remembering that what we do to others, we do to ourselves. That is the best description of the CC that I can provide.

The following chapters will be devoted to providing examples of how to embody The Christ Consciousness.

HOW MANY HIGHER SELVES DO WE HAVE?

If you could see a diagram of all the lives you have ever lived, past, present, and future, it would look like dots on a line that winds in the shape of a conch shell. You can see how the circular motion of the shell goes round and round, and then at the top, the shell turns back on itself into a winding downward spiral, and then back up again. This would represent the idea of no time as well as the dimensions that we exist in, simultaneously, and the unending nature of life cycles.

One can actually re-experience a particular lifetime as many times as they want through different perspectives, or focal points. Each time a soul revisits a lifetime, it will experience variations in that lifetime because the soul will make different choices during each iteration. The possibilities of what one may experience are infinite, and you might be very surprised to see yourself in another timeline having made different choices. These "revisits" help the soul evolve.

For example, what if you had married John instead of Paul? What if you had decided to become a pilot instead of a personnel administrator? What if you took that opportunity to be an exchange student during college and stayed in that country after you finished? These timeline variations exist and are very real. We get energy from all of our selves, from every lifetime, because all of our incarnations are part of us as One. We are usually not aware that this is the case because our consciousness is focused on this one timeline that we are on now, which we call our reality.

Some of the sci-fi movies have done a good job showing what it might be like to meet yourself in another moment of time, or as I would say, another dimensional version of yourself (focal point). There are versions of us in every dimension. Once we get to the versions of ourselves that reside in the dimension of the monad, consider that to be angel-like. Not quite merged back into Source, but very close. Those are called our highest selves. They are not better than us, or higher in importance than us, but they **are** of higher frequency, and therefore greater consciousness, than us. Those versions of us hold multidimensional realities without any confusion. They are who we will be, and already are, after we remember our Divinity. Our higher selves, the ones in between where we are now and our highest-self, are still evolving and journeying. If they were done journeying, they would return back to Source and relinquish their individual identities to be as One with Source. And after that, they might spring forth back out of Source to start it all again.

There is no beginning nor end to energy. It merely transforms. I forgot what scientist said that. Energy can neither be created nor destroyed, it only changes form. (After looking it up, I discovered that this is the first law of thermodynamics). Well there you go. It is that way with us in our incarnations and our energy.

Our highest-self (in the monad) provides the energy for all of our other incarnations, all the way down to 3D. We may even expand to lower than 3D, but I am not aware of that through my quantum healing explorations, so I cannot comment about it. The fascinating thing that I did discover through quantum healing is that we can experience someone else's life through a thing called imprinting. When the soul decides to incarnate, it may also decide to take on the imprint of another soul's life, to aid in the experiences of the upcoming life. An example, if I wanted to incarnate into a life and my soul plan is to become a great leader of the people in my country, I might imprint the life of another great leader, which becomes part of me as my own soul record of memories. This imprint becomes part of my Akashic Record as a life I have lived. There are many definitions of what the

Akashic Records are. I will tell you what I think they are. The Akashic Records are the energetic "memories" of every journey we have ever had or ever will have as aspects of Source. "The Akash" could be considered the memories of all souls, or the library of all experiences. Imprinting might give me the wisdom to become like that great leader without having to go through a bunch of other incarnations to learn how. Like hitting the "easy" button. It's like borrowing someone's awesome chocolate cake recipe when you've never made a chocolate cake before. You might spend a couple, if not many lifetimes, trying to figure out how to be a great leader or to make a chocolate cake, but it is easier to have the recipe imprinted so you as a soul can just get going on it.

This is happening more in this "time" of Earth's history because of the collective human expansion we call ascension. The vibration of Gaia is now 5D, and she is waiting patiently for us humans to catch up. We humans, our souls, are excited to get to 5D consciousness vibration as well, because we want to have heaven on Earth again. Imprints are not only gained before the incarnation happens either. Some people who are working on their vibration and really focusing on someone they would like to be more like can get an instant download (imprint) of the energy of that person's life. Parts of it, or the whole. This is done by soul agreement, and our higher selves usually make this agreement, unbeknown to us consciously. I am telling you about imprinting because we are finding more evidence of it in the quantum healing community. It seems these ascension times are really revving up the vibrations of All, which is what we want, and more of us are wanting to raise our consciousness faster. Imprints help us do that.

Our higher selves are us, in another dimension, and they contain more of our soul's energy than we do. Think of them as a more "evolved" us. They watch over us and communicate to us all the time. They communicate through our dreams, through songs, through people and books that we are attracted to read, they cause meetings and synchronicities to happen which guide us in certain directions. Directions that we planned before incarnating. They keep us "on track" so to speak. It is in their best interest for them to do so because after all, we are them and they are affected by what we are doing. It's not just us being affected by them. Our energy conveys to our higher selves.

Our higher selves, many of them, know of The Christ Consciousness energy. When we make the effort to connect with our higher selves, we are also connecting to The CC. Once we connect enough to The CC, and remember more of who and what we are, we become our higher selves. Not all of them at once, but like an evolution. We go to the next dot on the conch shell.

It is more important than ever that we understand that communing with our inner selves is key to higher vibrational energy. What do I mean by that? Let's go back to the concept that we all carry the spark of Source within us. That means that we are connected to everything and everyone that has ever been created, including our higher selves and the angels. How do we access them? In the past, we humans have been told that all of that was outside of us. We were told that we had to pray to the Divine, and that this was the only way to talk to God/Source.

What if that teaching is part of the separation games? To make us feel like there has to be a go-between us and the Divine? And what if now we can make these connections directly, because we are waking up to the fact that all is within us already? No go-between necessary. This is why I used the term "inner selves." All that we could ever seek; information, health, abundance, community…it's all right there, inside of us, and we must become aware of that in order to act like the creators we are, and manifest whatever we wish to see in our reality. Sounds like a bunch of spiritual bunk sometimes, but it is truth. The reason this concept is so difficult to grasp is that we have been programmed our whole lives to believe that we are separate from Source. Jesus knew there is no separation, and so he also knew he could heal a person by using his energy to match the person's perfect health vibration. Jesus did not see a sick person before him. He saw a version of the person before him that was perfectly healthy and assisted with merging the person's energy signature with the perfect health version. That is how energy really works. You cannot see yourself over and over again as sick and then expect that you will be well. You cannot hold the vibration of anger and sadness over a long period of time and expect that your body will experience perfect health. Those energies of anger and sadness are potent, low vibrational energies. When a human holds those energies in their bodies too long, they distort the cells of the body and cause dis-ease in the body. There are examples of people over time that had disease in their bodies, who began to make changes in their attitudes and started taking care of their bodies and emotions, and their bodies healed themselves. There are people who have had their conditions healed through the placebo effect.

How is that possible? It is possible because the people believed and received the energy of wellness. They did not need to have the actual drug to make a decision that their body would heal. And this placebo effect has been studied and proven to be real, so it's not a few random incidents that I am talking about here. Scientists continue to scratch their heads over this phenomenon, but I am more convinced than ever that it is the vibration of energy that we put out and receive that dictates what we can know and how we can feel at any given time. It's an internal job, for sure.

What does all this talk about physical and emotional health have to do with our higher selves? As I have stated before, we can access our higher selves to ask for wisdom and knowledge that we seek. The energies that we receive from our higher selves not only raise our consciousness and put us on the right path, but they can also transmute anything that we are experiencing that we wish to be done with. Jesus knew how to do this, and so he did it. We are learning how he did it. I can talk to you about how I did it, and this book will be ridiculously long. I'm suggesting you get your assistance and guidance from your higher selves, because they already know the path and they are just waiting for you to ask them for the knowledge.

How do you contact your higher selves? I'm going to rattle off a bunch of different ways, but this list is by no means a complete guide. First, you can meditate. Quieting your thinking mind, the left brain, allows you to become more open to hearing the messages of spirit and your higher selves. If nothing else, meditation will relax you and help improve your physical and emotional health. There are many ways to meditate. You can go onto YouTube and choose guided meditations which are labeled with their purpose and choose the ones that appeal to you. My personal favorite creator of guided meditations on YouTube is Steve Noble. Steve works with angelic energies, as do I, and so his meditations feel very powerful and effective to me.

You could be attracted to another type of meditation called "object meditation." This is when you place intentional focus on an object and notice everything about that object over a period of time. For example, your cat. You might notice the expression on the cat's face and the multiple colors within his fur as the light shines on some areas and not on the rest. You may notice that the cat has numerous facial expressions when it wants different things. You could decide to see how the cat seems when you pet it and consider its breathing as it lies next to you. The list of things you can become aware of during object meditation is infinite. Your object could be anything. I would choose something pleasant though, because things that gross you out will put you into your thinking mind rather than observation and quiet mind.

There are many forms of meditation, and you can look those up to figure out what type suits you the best. Practice and patience are the keys. Don't give up on meditation because you were only able to do it for a minute before your thinking mind broke into your peaceful space. That it totally fine! Meditation does not have to last an hour to be effective in contacting your higher-self. It may take more than a few times of practice before you do start communicating with your higher-self, so try to be patient with it.

The second recommendation is to consult with a psychic, a Reiki practitioner, a quantum healer, or another energy healer that can help you make the connection. Notice that I suggested going within first through meditation. That does not mean I think meditation is better, but I do think the sooner you start to trust that you have the power to go within, the quicker you will be able to just do it. You won't need outside help to get there.

Third, open up to hearing your higher selves. Set the intention and give permission for them to guide you and answer your questions. You will be amazed how quickly your intuition about things increases. Yes, that "gut feeling" you get, or knowing something without knowing why you know it, those are your higher selves communicating with you!

Fourth, find a way to exercise that allows you to release your thoughts and frustrations. When our thoughts become too many, our minds take over our focus and we are not as open to the communications from our higher selves. A simple walk over a short distance is a good start. Or if you are not mobile, you can do some stretching in your chair or your bed.

Fifth, start a dream journal and keep it near you when you sleep. That way, when you wake after dreaming, you can quickly write in it the content of the dream before you forget it. Those dreams are communication between you and your higher selves. Sometimes your guides and ancestors will contact you in dream state because that is when you are most receptive to messages. Either way, the dream journal will help you to interpret the messages. When you read the entries, feel into the meaning. Practicing this a little will lead to you deciphering the codes of dreams. You will get to the point where you say to yourself, "Oh, I know what that means!"

Sixth, trust that when you start seeing, hearing, feeling, and knowing messages from your higher selves that they are real. If you don't believe it is possible to communicate with your higher selves, then you will not believe the messages. How do you know that what you are receiving is true? Ask your body. Ask your body if the information you just received is true. If your body responds to the statement with tension, clenching, ill feeling like stomach upset, then the information is not true for you. If you feel lightness or excitement, then it is true for you. Your body never lies to you. It is the same for information that you receive outside of yourself like a newscast. Ask your body.

It will steer you right every time.

Okay, I feel complete in my sharing about the higher-self(s) with you. If you desire more dialogue about this topic, please feel free to contact me. My website (and contact information) is:

www.quantumexplorations.com

EXPECTATIONS AND THE CHRIST CONSCIOUSNESS

Have you ever planned to go to a party, and you spent weeks planning and preparing for this party, and when you got to the party it wasn't at all as good as you expected? There wasn't anything wrong, per se. The music was fine, the people were fine, and the food was tasty. You can't even put a finger on what made the party not what you expected. It just wasn't. I think we can all relate to the party analogy by inserting situations/events that were meaningful to us. It may be a relationship or a career, or even a whole family experience over time. In many situations, things don't go as we expect them too.

This is because we become attached to outcomes via expectations. We expect that if we do "A" and "B" that "C" will be the result. One plus one equals two, right? Not always. Let me give you an example. We have been taught that certain things we do will lead to having a good relationship with someone else. That all we need to do is these certain things, and then we can expect a positive outcome in the relationship. We become attached to that belief. We expect the formula to work. And then, we get baffled when it doesn't turn out that way.

What went wrong? Why wasn't it enough? and so on. What went "wrong" is that the other person was not receptive to having a relationship in the same way that you were, and so all those things you did, which should have led to a good relationship, did not work. People are people, and each of us has our own stuff going on, and that is just the way humanity works. We have free will. The moment you put an expectation on a person, or the weather forecast, be prepared to be disappointed.

To embody The Christ Consciousness, we need to let go of all expectations, save one. The one expectation that we can count on in all scenarios is that we will experience exactly what our life and soul need to experience, and it will happen in the exact right timing (when it will be the most beneficial for us to have that experience). There are no exceptions in the third dimension (3D). We can do the hokey pokey with manifestation techniques until the cows come home, and we still will not manifest something unless it is included in our soul plan potential, that we created and agreed to before birth. Some souls can and do choose to avert their soul plans by damaging their health or by suicide before their life plan (soul plan) can be completed. But they cannot cause something to happen in their life that is not in the plan in 3D. It would not benefit the soul's mission if we could just manifest our heart's desire, at will, in this dimension. What would be the point of journeying through all the hardships and challenges if we could just wave our magic energy wands and conjure the manifestation of what we expect would be bliss? Why even come to Earth if that were possible here, in 3D? It would be pointless, and the soul would not expand.

We come to Earth to expand our soul's experience, remember? Source gains ultimate knowing of itself through experience. As much as we are All powerful aspects of Source, we did not journey to the 3rd dimension, work our way up to the 4th dimension, with our sights of going even higher to the 5th dimension, to break the experience by knowing our magic in 3D. No, we came here in our limited vibrational capacity to create because we wish to experience what it is like to work our way up again to our Source knowing, and power. Up to the dimensions where we can instantly manifest our every thought and desire. And it's a good thing too that we can't do that in 3D consciousness!

Can you imagine, with our limited consciousness and our games of separation, how we would use that instant manifestation ability? There would be people walking around with toilets on their heads that they couldn't remove. Dirty toilets. And a whole host of other manifestations that would probably destroy the Earth.

The Christ Consciousness, related to expectation, would have us trust that we are always being taken care of by the forces of the Universe while we ascend, or, remember our true nature. In a situation where it appears that a person is not being taken care of, it is because that soul has this reality mapped out in their soul plan. They chose to experience abuse, or poverty, or some other fearful experience, and the Universe is giving them the experience that they have chosen. Our Universe, like Source, does not judge what we choose. We judge what we have chosen in our limited consciousness of 3D – 4D. Once we embody The Christ Consciousness, we know that everything we have chosen is perfect.

No need to judge it.

We work with what we have chosen and use it to move to the next highest thought about ourselves and each other. Replacing expectation with trust is the way to know that you are always connected to Source, you have a plan for yourself, and you are obviously a very strong being experiencing the density of 3D and still moving forward. That is success, no matter what else you "do" in your life.

Expectations are not the same as setting intentions, or goals. I would posit that setting a goal means that you are getting an inspiration from your highest-self (the oversoul), and this is why that goal is something you are interested in. Setting your intentions/creating goals is different from creating an expectation for that goal. The expectation of an outcome can make you feel that setting the goal was somehow wrong if it doesn't turn out the way you expected. For example, if I set a goal to start painting again during my free time, and I attach an expectation that I will sell my art, instead of merely enjoying the painting during my free time, I might be disappointed and feel that I have wasted my time if people won't buy my artworks. But, if I set the goal to start painting again and just enjoy painting because it brings me joy, then no matter if I sell it or not, it is a success. Can you see how we create our own distress through expectation?

The Christ Consciousness is the energy of love. Love of ourselves, and love of others. If we keep putting ourselves in places of distress, then we are not loving ourselves. If we place expectations on others, then we are not loving them. When we trust that the right people and the right circumstances for the evolution of our soul will come to us, then we are loving All, and that is embracing The Christ Consciousness.

HELPING

It is reasonable to think that helping one another is a basic tenet of embodying The Christ Consciousness. And it is. Helping yourself and helping one another is one of the best ways to be love. However, there is a fine line to walk with helping others. That line is when the help we are offering turns into control or dependency.

Sometimes we offer help to another because we can see, feel, or have been told that the person is struggling. An offer of help can be simple, as in, "is there anything I can do for you?" or it can be aggressive, "I know you can't pay your rent this month and so here, take this money." The first question shows your compassion and allows the person to decide if they need help or not. Then you can decide if you are able to provide the help that is needed. It is a mutually beneficial conversation. The second statement does not give the person the feeling that they have a choice. The choice to refuse the money is there, but the accusation that the person can't figure out their own problem is there too. That is not loving them. That is being controlling and potentially breeds resentment for both parties.

Dependency kicks in when we help too much. For example, the person keeps coming to you for money every time they cannot afford the rent. Maybe they do not work enough hours to pay the rent, or their spending habits cause them to be short each month, and they come to you for the balance. You keep giving it to them, every time they ask, because you think that is the loving thing to do. I understand why anyone would think that, but it is not actually the loving thing to do.

Not for either party.

It sets up a dependence on you, which over time, you may begin to resent. And for the person asking for the money, your continuance to give it to them signals your belief that they cannot generate money themselves nor come up with better spending habits. This scenario sets up an unhealthy, unbalanced relationship of energy exchange. You might think that the love of the person receiving the money is exchange enough. However, there is still the issue of loving yourself enough to not keep giving away your resources when that person could give more of their own energy to making more money for themselves, and also you are contributing to the energy of not believing in their ability to do so.

Energy exchange must be freely given and balanced for the relationship to be healthy. If one is giving (helping) far more than the other, then there is dependence happening with both parties. The party that gives too much is depending on the gratitude of the one receiving, and the one receiving is not believing in their own power to generate for themselves. Dependence is not love. Sometimes, the best way to help someone, and to help yourself, is to encourage the person to find their own strength and personal power in a situation. I would start with asking that person to list their strengths. Then ask them what they think might be the solution to their problem. Finally, I would be supportive and encouraging to that person as they work to achieve their own solution. Doing something for someone constantly, strips that person of their ability to find out that they can do it on their own. We might have good intentions, but the result is the same. And we do tell people what we think about them far more with actions than words.

Another thing about helping is that we must be aware of our motives to do so. Do we have extra time, energy, goods or money to give away to another? Yes, good. Now, do we feel called to help, has someone asked, or are we doing it because we need to feel better about ourselves and we think giving something might achieve that? How do we feel after we have given the help?

The secret to answering these questions is how we feel afterwards. If we feel resentment, then we were not "called" to give the help. We were asked and did it out of expectation or guilt. If we feel excited, and then later that excitement goes away, then we helped because we needed to prove to ourselves that we are good people. But if we helped, and it felt as easy as breathing, and we did not get an "energy high" out of it, but felt more like it was the natural thing to do, no accolades necessary; then we helped because we were called to. We just did it because we would have wanted someone to do it for us. Being "called to" help means that you have helped because you see the other person as an extension of you, as in Unity Consciousness, we are All One. You helped because you felt the sudden desire to, and you would hope for the same treatment if the roles were reversed. These intuitions, or "callings," are signals from the Universe that our higher selves want us to do something. They are not generated by thought. As I said earlier, they feel as natural as breathing, and no "thank you" is required by us afterwards. An example would be anonymous donations.

These examples might seem to be judgmental. I know it took me many years to stop being co-dependent, and to help others only when I was called to do so. There are three different energies associated with each example. One of them is the loving energy. The other two energies are associated with some type of need or belief (i.e. guilt, not good enough if I don't help, I owe it to that person because they are my family, etc.). Only you can decide the truth of your helping.

Remember I talked before about soul plans? Each of us has one. Sometimes the soul has placed difficulties in the path of itself (while incarnated) so that the self can find their own strength and pull themselves out of it. Kind of like the old saying, "pull yourself up by the bootstraps and keep going." If we do not allow that self to make their best efforts to pull themselves up before we step in and try to help, then we are robbing that soul of the chance to experience their own power. At the least, we are interfering with their soul plan, and that is not loving them. This includes the "disabled." They came to the world with their disability included in their soul plan. They need the opportunity to feel powerful and useful in determining their abilities. How will anyone know what they can do if they don't try?

    A final word about helping that was channeled by me from Archangel Metatron. I was struggling with a situation that a family member was going through. I had a lot of knowledge about the systems involved in the situation, and I threw all of my knowledge at this person to help them, because I love them. This family member did not appreciate me doing that. In fact, it may have caused more stress for this person. At my wit's end, I started meditating to ask what I could do next to help. I heard very clearly these words, "there is no more you can do for someone who will not grab the lifeline when it is thrown." If I had withheld my information until it was asked for, then both parties would not have felt offended. Or if I had withheld my information because I was holding a belief that my family member would figure it out on their own, but continued to be supportive of their efforts as they did so, then we both would have felt empowered by sharing the experience.

CREATION THROUGH THE CHRIST CONSCIOUSNESS

We all have desires, and desire gives us the hint that it is time to create. Desire can be considered the soul's communication with you that it is time to start something new in your life, or to do something. As far as I have known in my life thus far, there are two types of desires. One is the above mentioned. It comes from a place of you inside that knows what your essential self wants. The other desires come from society, or what is referred to as "social conditioning."

How can we know the source of our desires? This can only be done through introspection, or, in other words; searching inside yourself for the answers. Is the desire something you think you want, because you have been told by so many sources outside of yourself that you *should* want it? Notice I put the word "should" in italics? Anytime you think you *should* do something; you can consider that shitting on yourself.

"Should" is a word used by society to indicate expectation. We already talked about that. The real question is; what do you want? What action or creation will bring you joy? If you are considering your desire and you figure out that acting on that desire will bring you joy, then that desire is coming from inside of you. If, on the other hand, you discover that thinking about your desire reveals a *should*, then you may need to re-examine that desire. For example: I am a woman, I am married, and I have raised two children. I also work to earn a paycheck. If I have a desire to cook a meal every day for my family at 5pm because society has told me I *should*, and I believe it (that I should cook a meal every day at 5pm), then my desire is because of social conditioning. It did not come from a place inside of me that finds joy in cooking a meal every day at 5pm. Maybe some days I want to go out to eat at 5pm, and my highest joy would be to do that with my family. Or maybe I cook a meal most days at 5pm, because I enjoy cooking and providing my family with a home- cooked meal (most days).

Can you feel the difference in energy of those statements? Can you relate? I know many of you are thinking; 'well it's nice to go out to eat, but not everyone can afford to do that.' I agree with you, and I agree that it is unfortunate that everybody does not have the option to follow that desire to go out to eat. For this cooking example, I was assuming that I have the money to go out to eat, and that society may have convinced me that as a woman, I should cook a meal every day at 5pm.

Let's use another example about me that does not include money in the desire/choice. I am still a married woman with two children that works outside of the home in this example. Both of my children enjoyed sports during their school years. This choice involves me, as a woman, having the desire to play sports with my boys in the attempt to be closer to them and help them develop their skills (I am also an athlete). Or, do I have the desire to be "the team mom" where I sit on the sidelines and watch, bring fruit for the intermission, and not involve myself in their actual playing of the sport with which I am familiar? I know which role is expected of me, as a woman. I know which role most people in society would expect I should do. Luckily, while my boys were in school, I followed my greatest joy. I played with them. I played and coached baseball. I threw footballs and kicked soccer balls with them, even though I knew little about those sports. AND, I brought the fruit for intermissions when it was my turn and cheered for them from the sidelines. All of those things I did because I wanted to, not because someone expected me to. Yes, I cooked most of our meals every day at 5pm during the years when we did not have money to go out to eat. But that was because I preferred my cooking more than anyone else's in the house. I will say that my husband makes a few really good dishes and so he did the meal at 5pm sometimes.

The point is, I didn't play the sports nor cook the meals because society told me I *should*. I did it because I had the desire to.

Let's get real about something here…no one ever has to cook a meal. Groceries can be bought by both males and females, and most humans are capable of boiling water, making cereal, or putting a sandwich together. Creation through The Christ Consciousness means that we know what our greatest joy is, and we seek to take action based on that rather than creating because society thinks we *should*. I have a very high capacity to understand physics, yet I decided to create understanding of human behavior through social work for many years because that is what my soul was calling me to do. The work brought about joy for me. Much more so than crunching equations or fixing biomedical equipment. Society would have me believe that my choice of creation, working with people to better their lives, was a mistake because obviously a social worker makes much less money than an engineer. I have done jobs other than social work that have brought more money to me, and I can tell you without hesitation that they did not bring me more joy. And here comes another tenet of The Christ Consciousness. We can create for the purpose of survival AND simultaneously create for joy.

Living in this 3D – 4D we still have to make money for survival. That will not be the case for long once we reach the 5D vibrational reality. While we are still ascending/remembering how to be 5D, we can still create through our highest joy without sacrificing our survival. Pick up that paint brush if you like to paint. Crochet, write, conduct get-togethers, SING! Whatever brings you joy, and you feel the desire to do, then that comes from within.

How to test if your desire comes from you or from society? There are several ways. When you feel into the thing you want to create, do you hear your own voice speaking to you about it? Does it come into your thoughts often and unprovoked? Or, when you think of it, do you hear the voices of your parents, teachers, or some other person outside of yourself telling you why you *should* have the desire to create? Are you a member of a church that tells you regularly that you *should* do something/create? Has your family over generations always done certain things, and now you feel compelled to do them too? Maybe you come from a long line of family members who have joined the military. You feel compelled to follow this tradition but what you really want to do is go to a third world nation and help to bring technology or education to those people to improve their lives.

There are many, many people who follow society's prescription for happiness; they have the education, the big career and house, the fancy car…and many of them are miserable. There are many people who do not follow society's prescriptions of how to live life, and they find their happiness (rich, poor, and in-between).

Creation through The Christ Consciousness has nothing to do with history of any kind. Clear your mind by letting go of any thoughts with historical messages in them. Then quiet the mind and let your higher selves speak to you about your desires (meditation or silent reflection). Notice how you feel when considering each desire. Then allow yourself, one step at a time, to take actions towards your greatest joys.

YOUR BODY

All souls create a plan for their upcoming incarnation. This includes plans for the body that you will incarnate into. We choose our parents, and they choose us too, by soul agreement, which dictates what part of the world we will be born into and approximately how we might look. But the body is chosen by the soul to be the shape and condition that the soul feels is best to complete its life plan with. For example, if a soul wants to experience physical challenges in a lifetime so that it has the opportunity to remember that personal power lies within (a Christ Consciousness tenet), then that soul will choose to create a form for incarnation, its body, with a disability, or experience a debilitating sickness at some point during their incarnation. Or maybe have an accident that leaves their body physically challenged.

The point with this is that we know from the time before we are born, what our body will be like because we have chosen it and created it with our intentions, while not in form. We know if we will be tall and thin, or short and thick, smart, artistic, double jointed, athletic, attractive, have one foot longer than the other, etc. We also agree to every possible experience that we may have in our body. It is known, in spirit, that the body we choose may cause us to be criticized in the society we choose.

Why would we do that?

Because that experience gives the person the opportunity to overcome what society thinks about them. The soul already knows it is part of Source and is perfect. The experience of feeling "not-Source" can be had by incarnating in a body that is not regarded as ideal. Once the person realizes, or remembers, that they are perfect as they are, then they begin to accept The Christ Consciousness and embody it. They love their body for its gift of life.

We also create our bodies to be a communication system for us. It can tell us if our survival is at risk, what environments we prefer, and if we are working too hard (expending too much energy with thoughts and actions). Our bodies tell us if the food we eat is good for us, and how our emotions and behaviors are affecting our whole being. Our whole being consists of the four "light bodies," or "energetic bodies;" plus the physical body. The light bodies are: body, mind, emotional, and etheric (spirit). They appear outside of the physical body as "auras" to people who can see energy fields. Our physical body is impacted directly by the balance of our light bodies. If one is imbalanced, they all will become imbalanced eventually. Many people do not remember that we can create illness in our physical body if one of our light bodies is imbalanced. In truth, this is the only reason we experience illness; we have become imbalanced in one or more of our light bodies. But this is a quantum topic, and I want to keep to the basics of our human body communication at this time.

In spirit, we have created our bodies to communicate with us about all the aforementioned experiences. Our bodies communicate to us through feelings and health. If you make a statement about anything that you want to know is truth or not, and you pay attention to how your body feels when you make that statement, you can rely on your body to be your truth detector. It may give you a strange feeling in the gut, dizziness or fogginess in the mind, or even a headache, if the statement is false. In contrast, if the statement is true, your body may feel lighter, you notice an excitement or rush of energy, or even experience goose bumps. That is your body responding positively to the statement which indicates truth. Some people notice the hair on the back of their neck stands up when they hear truth. That is a confusing sign because it may also indicate danger. You will have to use that sign in the context of your surroundings. If you are in your kitchen, your spouse tells you something, and your little hairs stand up on your neck, you are probably not in danger. You are either joyful of the information or recognizing truth in it. Unless your spouse is wielding a knife and walking angrily towards you. Context is an important factor when considering what your body is communicating with you. Say you tune into the news (which we know can be slanted) and you notice that you feel "off" when you hear something. That could be your body telling you that what you just heard is not truth. Or it's not YOUR truth.

It may be someone else's truth and not yours.

Your body will communicate with you about your emotions. A good cry every now and then might make you feel a bit tired in your body, and that is normal. It is a release of energy from the body. But if you are stressing and crying often, your body may communicate that you need a break from those emotions by "catching a cold." We can't actually "catch" a cold. Organisms that cause illness are around us all the time. What makes a body sick is when we are very emotional over a period of time and our immune system becomes weak from all the adrenalin and cortisol the body must process from the stress. Your body gets overworked when that is constant. It does not work as it normally would. Then you are susceptible to all those illness-causing organisms that your body normally fights off with no problems.

Sometimes your body responds to heavy stress by becoming tired. Your muscles, brain and other systems don't seem to be going at top speed. This is your body "telling" you that it needs a break. It is telling you that your well-being will be compromised if you don't find a way to reduce your stress. People ignore these communications from the body and try to force the body into submission. Overindulgence in caffeine or other stimulants, drinking lots of energy shakes or telling themselves to "power through it" (mind over body). These things may help to get you to the finish line if you are near the end of a project, or you are moving house and you can't stop until your furniture is unloaded and the basics are unpacked. Those are scenarios where the "push" or the stimulant use are temporary. If it is the case that a person does this as a way of life, never quiets the mind, nor gets enough sleep, then the body will continue to degrade in functioning until you are forced to take time to recover. You may learn you have some kind of immune disorder or be diagnosed with chronic fatigue. You may also be told that your symptoms are all in your mind because doctors can't find anything wrong with you. What's really happening is your body finally said "no" to your pattern of pushing it too hard.

Lots of people learn to heal themselves physically by changing their patterns of stress. They stop worrying about things they cannot control nor change, and they take time for themselves to rest and recover from periods of intense stress. Maybe they even start a healthy exercise form like yoga or walking, which help the body and the mind to release stress energy. Have you ever heard of spontaneous remission? That's what I'm talking about. Even intense recovery of physical illness can happen once someone consciously decides to start taking care of themselves.

The degree of severity of illness tends to correlate directly with the amount of stress, worry, anger and fear that you subject your body to. Once a person decides to cease those energy investments, the body can heal and get back to its original functioning. People can also accomplish this through expanding their consciousness. I have been witness to some of my client's stories where they communicate with me that they listened to their higher selves and implemented the advice given during their session (quantum healing session), and poof! Their illness went away totally or was on its way to being resolved. Did I heal them through the session?

Hell no.

The clients allowed the messages from their higher selves to come through by altering their consciousness, and then they listened to those messages. They heard the advice given, and took advantage of it. All healing is self-healing, no matter what type of healing you go for. Western medicine, Eastern medicine, hypnosis, yoga, crystal energy work, holistic healing…it doesn't matter. Once you consciously decide you are going to heal, and you believe in the therapy that you chose, you will heal. You have maybe heard of the placebo effect? The placebo effect has been well documented in scientific studies. People who got the non-medicine treatment (placebo) had the same healing, if not better, than the ones who got the real medicine. Intention to heal is key.

Body-mind connection.

Conversely, if you don't believe in the method you chose, then your body knows that and thinks you plan to stay unwell. The body knows you. It gives you what you intend. It knows every intention that you have. It also knows if you are using illness to get attention, or to avoid some aspect of your life. Your body does not judge your intentions, it only gives you what you wish to experience. This is something to be mindful of. Before you go looking to try every form of healing you can think of, go within and figure out your intentions. How has your illness served you? Take responsibility for your illness. Don't blame your body or feel guilty about your intentions. It is okay to use illness to have an experience! That is your free-will, your right to choose. As with all The Christ Consciousness teachings, this goes back to remembering that you are a part of Source. You are a creator being. There cannot be a creation in your reality that is not of your making. This is not about blame. It is about becoming conscious of your creations. And in doing so, you embody The Christ Consciousness. Perfect health can be yours by the choosing.

My final word about the body is that you will benefit greatly by being grateful for it. Thank your body for all of the amazing things it does for you. Thank it for giving you the ability to manifest within it! Treat your body as you would a friend. Soothe it when it has been overtaxed. Rest it, and feed it good food. Exercise some and get plenty of hydration. Think of how much of our body consists of water!

The mind is part of and works in tandem with the body. Rest your mind. Give your mind information and experience that feels joyful to it. Give your mind exciting and interesting inputs. Let go of fear and worry. Your mind is intimately connected to your emotions and your body. If you keep putting yourself into situations where your emotions become frenzied, then your mind and body become frenzied too. It's all connected. Honor your body and listen to it. Become mindful and start dropping those things that harm your wellbeing.

FORGIVENESS AND RELEASE

These tenets of The Christ Consciousness are the ones that are going to help you raise your vibration and get you to 5D the quickest. Remember how I talked about social conditioning? One of the beliefs that society has crammed down almost all of humanity's throats is punishment. And when society is not trying to punish us for some transgression or other, we do it to ourselves. If you want evidence of this, take a look at the traditional media and social media and see for yourself how much of that content is about people doing bad things and how "unfair" the world is to this group or that group. It's rampant! And it needs to stop if we are to increase our vibration and embody Unity Consciousness. Souls did not come to Earth and forget who they are to live a perfect life! Quite the contrary, we came here to experience what it is to be **not** perfect, to learn what our soul wishes to express and to remember how to be unconditional love once again. Many souls agreed to come here and do really heinous things to others, because the others wished to experience that behavior during incarnation.

Nothing happens by accident. Think of the soul of Hitler. What I am about to say to you may make you want to throw rotten tomatoes at me, but I'm going to say it anyway. Hitler's soul came to be here, at the time that it did, and agreed to be the "bad" that he was, to raise the consciousness of humanity. You read that correctly. Hitler is an aspect of Source, like we all are, and he came here to do humanity a service by behaving so badly. Furthermore, the souls that died at Hitler's command chose that experience. They agreed to have it happen. Their souls knew full-well what would happen to them during the time of their incarnation with Hitler.

Why?

This is where it gets interesting. When souls journey into incarnation with each other, they often swap experiences over lifetimes. I am personally aware of lifetimes during which I was a soldier. I was a Roman soldier, and a Turkish soldier in at least two of my lifetimes. In both lifetimes, I was responsible for killing innocent men, women, and children. Does it make me feel happy to think I did those things? No. Am I making those choices in this lifetime? No. But my soul wanted to have journeys where it had the opportunity to experience all sides of separation from Source. Does Source care what I did in those lifetimes? Yes, and no. Source has had and always has compassion and love for whatever I am choosing to experience. But Source is not judging it. None of it. I covered this before. Unconditional love means that you love someone completely, no matter what they do. You may choose to stay away from someone if they hurt you, but you don't stop loving them ever. Why would Source judge itself for its explorations through us? Why would you judge yourself for having varied experiences in a low vibrational reality?

Some of you will say, "it's in this bible, or _____ sacred text, that if you do x,y,or z, it is unforgivable." Who wrote those texts and bibles? Humans. How many instances can we find where a story was told so many times that it lost its original meaning? Or maybe that story has been intentionally distorted in its meaning so that it could be used for someone's own purposes? We know that scientific research studies can be manipulated to return results that back just about any contention. Science is not absolute. This is why so many scientific theories are rarely "proven." They remain theories until another scientist comes along and disproves them, or adds to them. What makes the writings of humans any different? And maybe the authors of so many religious texts had the best intentions for humans in-mind, but their limited consciousness did not allow them to understand their own prophecies. Some food for thought.

Let's get back to souls choosing the roles of good and evil. We do it to swap experiences, for ourselves and for each other, which is a kindness and a service we give to one another. The other reason we do this is to expand individually. How can we know that we choose the light if we have never experienced darkness? How can a soul have wisdom about knowledge if it does not have the corresponding experience? How can Source know everything about what it is like to be not-Source if its aspects are not allowed to experience it as far as it can go?

Contrast.

We need contrast to make individual consciousness decisions. If I experience killing innocent people in one lifetime, and I did it out of the consciousness that I was defending my country, and then cross over to the higher vibrational realities and my soul realizes that killing someone for my country is not how I wish to be, I may need to go through several lifetimes more until my embodied consciousness remembers that I don't choose to kill anyone for any country. I would begin to understand, while embodied, that self-preservation is the only acceptable reason to kill someone. If someone tried to kill me or someone else, I might kill them first to preserve a life. Self-preservation or saving a life are the only reasons I could imagine myself killing anyone, and I would take no pleasure in doing so. My consciousness has grown over lifetimes, and my decisions about killing have changed dramatically from those lifetimes as soldiers. My soul has expanded, and I may yet come to the point of embodying The Christ Consciousness enough to where I would not kill anyone for any reason.

Like Jesus.

Speaking of Jesus, why didn't he remove himself from the cross? Why did he allow himself to be captured in the first place? I have a theory about that and it has to do with the topic of forgiveness and release, and so I will share it with you. My theory includes the belief that Jesus was a higher consciousness being incarnated on Earth, who never went through the Veil of Forgetting. He never lost memory that he is of Source while incarnated. Jesus came to Earth as a service to humanity, to share

The Christ Consciousness with us. Humanity was floundering with their inability to remember who they are, aspects of Source. Jesus took on the mission to help humanity remember. Unfortunately, those humans that sought to keep other humans from remembering their true selves did not want Jesus to succeed in his mission. Those that wanted to maintain power and control over the masses recognized the power of Jesus' words and the power of the energy that he offered humanity, so that humanity would find that power within themselves.

Jesus spoke of unconditional love and that we are all One (Unity Consciousness). He told us that what we do to others, we also do to ourselves and God. He also told us that we could do all that he could do, and more. Jesus spoke of the dimensions when he taught us that God has one house with many rooms. And so, those that were threatened by the teachings of Jesus decided to have him killed. As if blasphemy could be any worse than murder (Barabbas). But that was the excuse. Why did Jesus allow it? He could turn water into wine, cure the blind, and bring back the dead. My theory is that Jesus tried very hard to complete his mission but could see that most of humanity was not ready to embrace The Christ Consciousness. He probably knew that even if he freed himself from the Romans, that he would be hunted and equally persecuted by some other group that didn't want to lose their power and control over humanity. And Jesus, knowing that there is no real death, allowed himself to be killed physically.

The biggest take away from that part of Jesus' life is his final gift to humanity. After being tortured, he was dying on the cross and asked God to "forgive them, for they know not what they do." Jesus spoke of forgiveness and to treat others as you would be treated his whole adult life. And at the most harrowing moment of his life, his actions matched his teaching. The man didn't just talk and preach to others. He became the example for them. Jesus knew, while embodied, that there is no real death, only transformation of the energy of the soul. But he was also in human form, with human emotions. To go through all of that and still forgive the ones responsible for murdering him; that is the ultimate expression of The Christ Consciousness embodied. Jesus planted the seeds of The Christ Consciousness so that we could find it within ourselves.

We have learned from Jesus and other ascended masters that it is important to forgive ourselves and others. But why? There are three reasons that I know of.

First, we are all just souls having a journey which we agreed to. Those that made agreements with us to do harm to us while embodied, have done so because we asked them to. We have lots of learning and growth to experience through these interactions and exchanges.

Second, forgiving yourself means that you can be forgiving of others. You trying to make yourself more "right" by making others "wrong" is not the kind of energy that will raise your vibration, nor your consciousness. Trying to find the wrong in others is a low-density energy form and only leads to more anger and resentment for both parties. Instead, make yourself right by accepting that you are not perfect in your human form, and forgive your own past transgressions. Know that you can never fail or be wrong in the eyes of Source no matter what you do. You are merely on a journey.

And third, forgiving the self and others feels better than the alternative. Anger, resentment, and hate do not feel good. These emotions harm the body and are felt by the soul. The soul's ultimate mission is to remember itself, as Source, while embodied. It wants you to feel joy and love. It wants you to overcome the illusions of separation. When something feels good to the soul, whether it makes sense to your mind or not, do it. If you find that you cannot forgive no matter how hard you try, try being ready to forgive. Being willing to open yourself to a higher state of consciousness allows The Christ Consciousness to be known within you. It is already there in your heart center. Reach for it. Ask your guides, angels, The Christ Consciousness, your ancestors, Jesus, the ascended masters, Source, or even nature to help you with it. Be patient with yourself and you will get there. You will come to know the power of forgiveness. The power of love will overcome anything, and you will be free.

Release! Once you have forgiven yourself or someone else, the next step is to release that experience back to the universe, God/Source, or to the light. This is done by imagining the experience as if it were a balloon filled with the energy of the event(s), and you simply let it go. You watch it as it rises up and away from your energy fields. If you can, add some gratitude for what the experience has taught you about yourself. You must remember that the saying about "forgiving is a gift to yourself" is true. The reason that it is true for All, or a universal truth, is because it shows that you have recognized your power to transmute anything. You are no longer attached to it because you are releasing it. You have freed yourself and the other from the burden of continuing the energies of the event in your energy fields, your reality. By doing this, you allow all new energies into your fields to create what you wish for in your life. Energy can neither be created nor destroyed, it can only change form. When you release the energy of a traumatic situation, that energy can now be turned into something more loving. And you get to feel lighter because you are not toting it around with you anymore.

Embodying The Christ Consciousness is accepting Unity Consciousness. That means that no matter how many times we forget that we are All One, we can, in the very next moment, remember again that we are. When we look outside of ourselves and notice another soul or group of souls that are behaving "badly," we can re-cognize that they are indeed "us" acting out another form of experience. They may be behaving poorly in our current reality, but that is not who they are in truth. Then, instead of thinking thoughts of punishment and retribution, we can energetically send them our love and our hopes and prayers that they will see their own light in this current focus of reality, as we have. We believe in redemption, right? What if we could help that process along for another by recognizing the light within them? What if we could forgive because we know how easy it is to lose our own way sometimes? What if that forgiving energy you have sent to another through your thoughts is just the thing that shifted their consciousness? The spark of Source energy, love, that you gave to another was the turning point for that soul to see their own spark of Source. Yes, we are each THAT powerful. Love is the only frequency that can bring darkness into light and change all of our thoughts about our fellow travelers. Just as Jesus reminded me of who I am in the one moment our eyes met, you too can give that gift to another by seeing Source in every single person you meet. When we do that, there is no need for forgiveness. There is no need for vengeance. There is only respect in allowing others to come to their remembrance of their light when the time is right for them to do so. We keep moving forward in life, minding our own business and loving the best ways that we can, and we trust that the "others" will follow when they are ready. We can be the example. We can carry Jesus' torch, his mission, and help humanity rise. Releasing others from your expectations frees you to live your best life at the same time that you are being the example. With love and reverence for All.

GRATITUDE

We in the spiritual community, talk a lot about having gratitude. The saying goes that the universe hears you when you are grateful for something and sends you more of it. I believe this is true. Universal forces are energies that act as a bounce-back to whatever energy you put out to it. You throw the ball (your energy), and the universe bounces it back. Universal forces give us more of the same that we send out. The stuff gets amplified also. I can't say why that is. I don't know why. I can guess that, like our bodies, universal forces are set up by our souls to provide direct feedback of what we are creating. This would serve to help us remember that we are creating our realities.

An example I like to use is a trip to the grocery store. I have noticed over my 54 years on this Earth, that when I go to the grocery store and I'm in a hurry, people are impatient with me. If I go while I'm angry, I encounter angry people. But, if I go while I am not in a hurry to be anywhere else, I take my time shopping with my list, and I am considerate of the others trying to get their shopping done, then I encounter much of the same. There are occasions, when I am in a good space, that turn up a stressed-out shopper near me, or a checkout person who is having a really bad day. I find that in those instances I am not bothered by the energies of those people. Their energies do not overtake my good mood. I also find those occasions as good opportunities to be kind and help spread my good energy. It is really difficult for someone to be mad at you when you smile at them! And one smile from you can make a person's shitty day turn around.

Gratitude is a vibrational energy that carries the same frequency as love. When you are being grateful, you are acknowledging what is going right in your world. Look around you, wherever you are, and find things that you usually take for granted and imagine they are not there anymore. How would you feel about that? How about the air that we breathe? What if we didn't have that? And yet we assume that the air is there and will always be there without being grateful for it.

There is always something we can find to be grateful for. If you cannot find something, then I would suggest you start trying to do it consciously. And give it your best efforts. The big mistake that humans make is looking for things to go wrong in their world. We can get ten compliments and one criticism, and most of us will focus on the criticism. Learning to include gratitude as a daily ritual shifts this tendency. This is a tenet of The Christ Consciousness. If you practice being something that is vibrationally higher than something else, you will become that higher frequency. If you practice a low frequency, you will become it. It's also some law of energy that when an atom is bombarded with a higher frequency of atoms or lower, the original atom will take on that frequency. It will be like breathing, your ability to feel grateful, as you practice it. And then the universe will send you more things to be grateful for!

THE ALL

I have stated this numerous times and I will say it a thousand more; **each one of us has the spark of Source within us, and we can connect to it at any time.** Everything and everyone that has ever been and ever shall be is right there inside of us for accessing. We access The All without knowing it when we are consciously or unconsciously creating. If you think that there is any idea or song that has been written down that has not come from Source, from one dimension or another, then you are still mostly in forgetting consciousness. That means you still do not remember your connection and you are creating your realities unconsciously. This is fine, and nothing to worry about. Everyone remembers in their own time.

The All is the information, memories, and energy of Source. Source's consciousness, if you will. There is nothing that cannot be remembered or recreated. Nothing we create is entirely new. Just look at fashion. It recycles. Yes, "new fashions" tend to have a slightly different flair or color variation. But, if we go through history, fashion can be seen as creative recycling. It is the same with science, relationships, and everything else you can imagine.

Discarnate souls like to help incarnated souls who engage in the same interests. They will touch our consciousness with their own to provide "inspiration" for our efforts. This can happen in dream time and so most don't remember the connection. I promise you that if you are trying to create something similar to another person's work, or expound on their work, all you have to do is get your energy in alignment with theirs and you will tap into their energies/creativity. This person could be dead or alive, it doesn't matter. When we decide we want to be like someone, it is because we have an affinity for their energy. We look at their pictures and their creations, or we listen to interviews with that person, and before you know it, we may even start behaving like them. This means we have aligned with their energy signature. Because we have access to The All, we can align with the energy of anyone. We are co-creating with that soul through this alignment.

The All will provide knowledge about anything we wish to become, create or learn IF this does not interfere with our soul contract. For example: I want to become a better painter. I open myself to the energy of Rembrandt and da Vinci because I am interested in painting figures and faces that are realistic. The All will not set me up to work with an artist whose specialty was Cubist or Abstract. The All will provide the energy of Rembrandt and da Vinci because I have placed my focus on them. Now, if it is not in my soul contract to become a famous painter, but I have dedicated most of my time and resources to painting, then The All may allow me to continue this connection to a point, but I will probably never attain the level of creation as Rembrandt and da Vinci did. I will eventually be redirected towards my soul path by something like poverty, which would force me to start using my talents in a way that is consistent with my soul plan. Understanding that The All provided me with exactly what my soul was asking to experience, through my soul plan, is embracing The Christ Consciousness.

The All wishes to honor your soul contract and so it will not give you something that will take you away from it. For instance, I could wish, for most of my life, to be a rock star. I may have learned how to play musical instruments and practiced over the years. But my soul wants me to work on family relationships and being a rock star might derail that plan. The All will allow me to have the information needed to play music as a hobby, but not the higher-level information and talent to become a rock star. That is loving; knowing All and giving only what is asked for by the soul. Our oversoul is in higher vibration, remember, than our incarnated self. Our incarnated self sometimes wants things based on egoic desires rather than soul desires. Once we start listening to the soul's desire, then we embody The Christ Consciousness and start to work with The All to obtain the information, skills, and be supported in that journey. We recognize that our other human desires are valid, but we want more out of life than the desires of the ego. We may even realize that we are happier since we have let go of the egoic desires because we are doing what we came to Earth to do. Our consciousness has connected to the oversoul consciousness (otherwise known as embodying our higher-self), and they are very happy about that!

I have had a few conversations with The All, in meditation and during hypnosis. In a way, you could say I was talking to God/Source's consciousness. It felt more expansive than any other collective I have worked with or the angels. Humans call God "The All Knowing," so maybe I have just truncated the name. I only know that when I asked this collective to tell me their name, I heard, "The All." And I have been calling this energy that ever since. Again, I am being reminded by my guides that it doesn't matter what I call it because I have been trying to explain about it. I have gratitude for it. I know The All has my back in every way possible, and I trust it.

The All is also a term I use to mean all of humanity. What serves one, serves The All. We are all One in another dimension, and we are all One right now. There is no separation, only the illusion of it.

What I do to you, I also do to myself.

CONCLUSION

We are all souls having a human journey within a creation, in a dimension that has served us to know separation. Our higher selves have decided to go back the other way into remembering that we are All of Source. We have never separated from Source completely, no matter what one or many of us has done. Source and The All are within us, always. We forgot who and what we are so that the journey seems real to us. And now we are awakening from the dream, the illusion that separation from Source is an actual thing.

Each one of us is a perfect creation. Source makes no mistakes, and it does not judge itself. Source is pure love, and so are we all. Source has provided a higher-knowing of itself that surrounds us in our journeying, and we can call this The Christ Consciousness. It is the energy that Jesus and other ascended masters brought to Earth, to ignite within us the memory of who we are. The Christ Consciousness can be understood through discussions and examples. It can be embodied, by each of us, through our own beliefs and behaviors. The first step to embodying The Christ Consciousness is becoming open to releasing everything you ever thought or believed about Source, if it no longer fits with your truth, being open to new truths, or expanding on your current truths, are the best courses of action toward grabbing the energy of The Christ Consciousness and allowing it to flow through you.

You can never fail at life. Life incarnate is an opportunity to play out your soul's plan for expansion, to remember what it already is after experiencing more of what it is not.

We can always find ways to be more loving, especially to our bodies and our whole selves. And it goes without saying that we can always show more love to each other. It is my belief that the second coming of Christ is not a reference to another human. It is a reference to all humans. We each have the opportunity to realize The Christ Consciousness. We need to be patient with ourselves and with others as we take on this journey to The CC. We could forgive more and be offended less if we can see life as an opportunity for souls to play out their contracts and their missions.

We humans have help, every moment of every day of our lives. We are never alone. We have angels, guides, ascended masters, Source, ancestors, ET's, The Christ Consciousness, the universe, and The Earth, Gaia; all conspiring to help us meet our soul's journey with love and support. All we need to do is quiet our thinking minds and ask them for help. Because we incarnated on a free will planet, we must ask for them to help. And they will help, always, in a manner consistent with our highest good. Look for the signs and synchronicities and know that these are interventions. They are communications and assistance. There are neither accidents nor coincidences. They may not give us what we want, but they will send us what we need if we ask.

Being grateful for All the good in your life is a great way to get more. Understanding that the "not good" in your life has happened to serve you will help you learn to forgive. We don't know what another soul has asked to experience and most of the time we are unclear what our own souls asked for. Trust that your soul had very good reasons for the experiences you are having. Trust that you are an all-powerful creator, and whatever didn't kill you, you will grow stronger from. And finally, trust that there is no real death. The loved ones that we have the illusion of losing are never far away from us. They are never disconnected from us. We miss seeing them, touching them, and interacting with them for sure! Grief is only the illusion of separation, but it feels very real. The good news is that if you learn to go within and reach out to them, be silent and listen for them, you will know that they are still with you.

There are many incarnations of your soul's energy in many universes and in all dimensions. All of them are you, and you have the ability to communicate with them, to bring those aspects of yourself back into One, the highest-self. I say that paying attention to all the versions of you; healing energetic emotional wounds and recognizing all of the abilities you have over lifetimes, is equal to embodying your highest-self. We can bring down heaven to Earth by being the highest versions of ourselves. When we shift our creations by accepting All that we are, over all of our journeys, then we will find ourselves living a 5D reality. And from what I hear, that is like heaven on Earth!

You have the power and the knowledge of The All within you. Source knows you are coming back to the One through Unity Consciousness. In some dimension of the highest vibration, you are me and I am you. When we start to see all of humanity that way, we can be each other's best friends, energetically speaking. The energy of one can be felt by another across the planet. Send out your love in the best possible ways you can. Hold the highest visions of yourself and others in your consciousness. Set boundaries and protect yourself when you need to, but don't close the door on humanity because we are going to remember, as a collective, who we are. We are going to stop living through fear and the illusions of separation and we are going to be 5th dimensional beings, consciously.

I love all of you. I hope this has benefitted you in some way. I'll see you in 5D!

www.ingramcontent.com/pod-product-compliance
Lightning Source LLC
LaVergne TN
LVHW052002060526
838201LV00059B/3792